You are my Hope.

Abigail Remmer

Illustrations by Diana Stefanescu

All my love.

Why did you leave, why did
you not stay and fight?
Where is your loyalty
to the King? My very
own huntsman, someone
to splinter their way through

my wildwood. To navigate
their way through these foxgloves,
these Ivy's and these nettles.
I am scared that your vines
will grow out,
like a headless willow.

I cannot taste the fruit
that you now hold out,
my taste buds bitter with
longing and rejection.
Why did you leave me, why
did you not stay and fight?
Where is your loyalty
to the King?
There to tend to your
forest of the forsaken.

Please Brother,
stand up for what is right.
There was once a fire
that burnt between us,
extinguished by our fears.

Leaving a smoke so thick,
we can longer see each other.
And even after all these years,
you are still
the Prince of my dreams.

O brother, what have you done?

My first invasive thought today was the image of you.
I dreamt of you in my sleep.
I woke up to slog myself to the toilet,
and in the brief 30 seconds where I fall onto the porcelain seat,
and my eyes stay closed to keep slumber intact,
I am thinking of you.
Saying your name aloud hydrates my throat
and prepares me to drag myself back
to my recuperative master,
to dream of your lips some more.

-A world gone wrong

I wish you could see the boundless Universe in His smile,
but it's okay because in His car all the while,
He tells me that I am the night star so young and free.
I am crying because He will not stop lying to me.

-Honestly

You are a siren in the dark.
The bringer of light and clarity.
I think you need me, just like I need you.
If the darkness becomes too much,
I will softly sliver up the Rocky Mountains and knock on the doors
of every witch hut concealed by the clouds.
With my passion and my energy,
I will never relent.
I will find you a cure.
I will banish your fear for this love of ours.
When we fall into bed and you wrap your hands around my throat
like a necklace,
I will thank you and peel your soul from your body.
With elegant efficiency, you shatter beneath me into sharp, shard-like
fragments, ready for me to put you back together again.
But all the king's horses and all the king's men
will never be able to put you back together again.
So, I will be your maker.
I will take the risk.

-Husky embrace

Abigail Remmer

I have lost my mind trying to figure you out.

−*Running a mile a minute*

I want to hurt you for your negligence.
How could you leave when I needed to eat you alive?
I'd eat you for dinner and dance in the glow of
the hellish flames that I create from my crime.
Right person.
Wrong time.
I dream of us in a seedy motel room,
your lithe body writhing against the limits of your self-control.
You think you're disciplined until I show you the way,
I'll make you burn up with love until you beg me to pay.

You hit me where the goddamn heart is.

Telling myself to forget you
is like telling the tide to go back in;
pointless and beyond the realms of
my Power.

A missed meeting
a chance encounter.
Just one stare
just one pointed look.
Just one forest fire
deep within her
Now you have a
section in this book.

-IOS

Abigail Remmer

I miss the electricity,
that feeling of anticipation and numb hands,
sweaty palms and shaking legs.
I feel it only with you.

-Maybe I will feel it with him too

Suffocate me and violate me,
halt my breathing and stagger my heart.
I want your foreign hands weighing me down.
Oh baby, when I see you,
I just want to smell you.

-Nobody but you

I don't want this dream to be over.
I've left you crying and creasing,
listening to my story.
Sometimes I feel like I'm flying in circles
around the sting of the sun.
The sun that reminds me of you.
Fiery, powerful and the bringer of light.
Brown feathers lay on your head,
green orbs rest in the hollows of your eyes.
Soft whispers sound your S's,
God formed your fingers by hand.
He sculpted every single part of you,
your sharp cheekbones,
your ghostly complexion,
every atom in your body
that deserves only a red carpet,
and a passionate embrace.
I will rise from my sky,
creating the most beautiful life
for us to breathe in and cope.
Oh, mein Liebling,
you are my Hope.

-Please do not let me down

With every venomous word I say to you,
the old me digs her talons deeper into my chest,
ripping at flesh and scratching at the bone.
Some days I want to give in, but I don't.
I would give anything for you to look at me like you love me.
I think I am in love with a memory.

I can see you standing there waiting for me.
I am on the dark edge of the town, shrouded by the woods.
Come a little closer and dance with me,
I think I might have been sleepwalking with cards in my hands.
Shake me from side to side, I have our meeting place autopiloted into my memory.
On the edge of town where no one can find us, you say to me again and again.
I can smell the smoke on your jacket and the taste of vodka on the bed of your tongue.
Your heart is so pure and heavenly, you could lead a thousand disciples to their deaths in pursuit of a reward from you.
You f*** us all over and leave us dying for your touch.
There are magic and danger on your lips and a wicked, dark agenda in your eyes.
Eyes that match the crisp summer leaves.
The sun is beginning to set to the West and for a minute the sky is pink and purple and blue, but its angelic colours are in no comparison to you.
When I awake,
I am still waiting for your love.
I can feel my body getting cold.
I tried to release you to the wind,
but you make me so high that I just can't find my mind.

-*Paper cuts and cigarette burns*

I have recurring dreams where I call out to you for help.
Either you ignore me, or you are never there.
Why won't you save me?
Why are you not here now?
I hope that when it came down to it,
that you would save me.
I know that you wouldn't.
I don't believe that you would come.

-Heartbreak in the diner

Pain can be a great motivator and a great source of creativity, but so can happiness and hope. Hope and happiness get the most attention in my life because they inspire me the most. I believe that you need to fight for your fairy-tale, (with a little help from the Universe!) If you have a love for yourself and you have an awareness of the beauty of your own soul, a soulmate is a wish granted, a fling is a fun thrill, and unrequited love is just a stranger on the street that you don't need to care about.

I wanted to draw our initials
on the wet condensation of the window,
but it's stuck to the outside.
Just like you, it is unreachable.
Another sign…

-A wish granted

Abigail Remmer

Time is illusory.
If it were real,
I would choose
every single second
with you.

You may have locked me in the Prison of Pain
but you shower her with Lockets of Lies
and Rings of Romance.
She is the true prisoner.

-Marriage and Murder

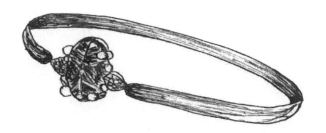

Abigail Remmer

I do not hate you,
for hate will pull me into the shackles of darkness.
I do not like you,
for liking takes no sides.
I do not love you,
for love will race me into a war I cannot win.
I choose to think not of you,
for that will bring me Peace.

-Acceptance

Every time we are together but cannot truly be together,
a part of my soul dies.
Being so close to you without your touch is like death kissing my
body.
Every sunrise, I see you in my vision.
Every sunset, I muse about our conversations.
Every moonlight wonder is spent on the very thought of you.
You merrily slip into my dreams with your childish grin and your
angelic light.
I know your pupils dilate when we are together,
even though you do not feel the same as me.
In my dreamy paradise, we can be together.
I can touch you how I want to,
speak to you how I want to,
and love you how I want to.

Just.

Like.

That.

You pulled out a dagger and slashed my heart right out.
Right there in the hallway.
The fleshy organ falls from my ribcage and lands with a thud onto the floor.
The blood seeps from my chest, and my eyes and my ears.
I am a Blood Red River.
But just like the wounded wolf in the forest, I have sustained many injuries in my life.
You have made me Immortal.
So please, try again.

-The lion and the sheep

Death grazes my soul and permeates my view,
I can see the incandescent flaming fire in you.
Hazel planets and a messy furrowed brow,
exclaim to me, 'live, I am here now'.

-You found me

You dragged me halfway to hell.
I was your burden to bury.
I wanted to chase you until you were exhausted.
I wanted to blind you until you saw me.
You will never be free of me because my blood is on your hands.
You are living a lovely lie by my grace.

-And you say Hamlet is a bastard

I thought that you were the only one that could knock the wind out of me, destroy me, bruise my coccyx and batter my heart.
Then he came along, and what a wild wind he was.
The Wildest Wind.

I am so grateful that today you and I held hands at the beach. The sun was shining brightly in the corner of my vision. The sea crashed near us as the waves kissed our feet. You rolled your jeans up as we tangled our fingers together. The beach is in Bali, or maybe somewhere in LA. There's a seafood restaurant behind us with honeymoon tables. You smile at me and I smile even wider. I am so grateful for how loved and special you make me feel. You make me feel like life is a paradise and you are the Heaven. Feeling your skin makes me happy. I am so grateful that we spent the day together on the beach, in the sun, just us two. Life is good.

-Law of Attraction

Green eyes meet green eyes.
You bite your bottom lip and
a tsunami builds inside of me.
Battery acid boils in my brain.
Rub that pen between your fingers
just a little bit faster.
I need to calm the lion.
Faster, just a bit faster.
'Hi'
I just die.

-Sweet relief

When you left me, I could taste my demise like a chocolate bar.
Sweet.
Regretful thereafter.
You are the rush of dopamine that excites and pleasures but
disappoints and crashes.
You were not worth it but clearly,
I was colour-blind; red flags all looked like green to me.

-Human chocolate cake

She desires a butcher.
He killed my wife, said he.
I believe he did, said she.

-La Douleur Exquise

My perception of you does not align with reality.

Limerence.

You differ in a million ways to what I thought you were.

Limerence.

It's unfair for me to project this fantasy so unreal.

Limerence.

How do I rid myself of it?

How sweet and crisp the midsummer night air is,
the smoke signals flittering into view.
Please come back to me,
I need that sugary vision of you.
I cry and toil and mourn,
from this embrace
of arms wrapped in thorn.

-But now I'm free of your Thorns and I can feel the Insurgence of Hope.

Abigail Remmer

How can I possibly get to know you?
I don't even know all of myself yet.

Fight for it.
Fight for your power.
Fight for those who cannot fight for themselves.
Fight for yourself.
Fighting has made me the rough diamond I am today.
Fighting will make me the shimmering star tomorrow.

In the tulip fields,
I will read a love poem
crafted just for you.
I will feel you feel me.

With you
I don't want to pretend or hide.
I am not afraid.
I will always tell you the truth.

-Knight of Pentacles

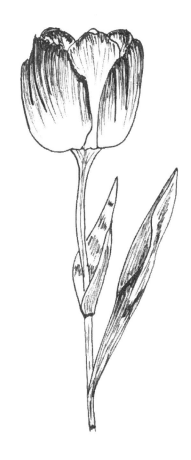

You could be my lover from another planet, flying through the constellations and feeling the frequency floating through the air.
I can't get enough of your twisted love language like an enigma code.
The emotion that I'm feeling is all mine, and never yours.
People are never as good as we paint them to be in our heads, but even at a distance so cruel, I know your love will be too much. Our bodies are intertwined with the invisible red thread with small golden beads that use a Morse code to spell out our future as soulmates.
The thread is invisible to those around us.
I am destined to ride this path alone, and I cannot have a puncture in the tyre of my temple.

When I close my eyes, I will fly us to the moon, and we will lay on the grey and black craters of the sphere and point out our star signs. Star-crossed lovers.
We will name the stars we do not know.
Their twinkling beams fighting with your dashing smile and your luminous eyes.
I don't want to open my eyes. Is this a dream? I ask you.
Of course, it is we are on the moon and we are together, how can that possibly be real? You say.
Because I am a fool, and I have limitless Hope. I say.
You grab my hand and I can feel the light of the morning sun attempting to disrupt our vast paradise. Stroking my hair, I can see the shimmer from the stars cast a shadow on your dark eyes.
I don't want to let you go. Please don't make me let you go.
Then don't, you say. Have hope, close your eyes and dream of the paradise where we will share a lifetime together.

-Alien lover

Abigail Remmer

Raised on coloured water and mud pies,
I don't feel the same anymore.
I realise,
I don't have to be alone.

-Pink shimmer

Oh, my beautiful manipulative Sir.
Every day you get closer to ruining me,
and every day I get closer to letting you.
How have you tamed the lion so quickly?

You have been hurt and you have hurt others.

-You will seek your own punishment

My love started in the gentle arms of my father;
the first person to ever hold me.
A young child shouting 'I'm following you so please don't make me fall,
for I will have soon grown and wrapped my vines around you that now stand so tall'.
Sometimes you are too heavenly for my mortal eyes to see,
so please be kind and understanding whenever you think of leading me.

One day, I will share my stories in the seven cities of bliss,
and I will spend a lifetime recounting the memories I now miss.
On one Midsummer's night, my journey will lead me to a Bethlehem stable,
and I will tell the innkeepers the divinity of your fable.
I will tell them how you have led me with your love so pure and true,
how just like their righteous and holy saviour, I must now follow you.
'Who told you this walk with my heavenly father would not be hard?
For every part and parcel and persecution upon you will be barred.
This cup that is poured out for you is the new covenant in my blood,
my very existence has brought you the grace to stand where you are now stood.
How many everything's can you seek and how many everything's can you hold,
for I will muster up my merciful might to transpire your soul into glittering gold.'

He will guide you towards the light with no deception in his ways to speak,
rather he will care for your woes and nurture you until the end of the sunset peak.
I hope you see the guiding light of the heavy Northern Star,
for all Three Wise Men will take note of the father that raised the bar.
Your journey will take you from the Far East to the Far West,
and in the face of that, you will laugh at Life's final test.
For that, wickedly wildwood will spindle out its small voice,
'I hope I will always be my father's rejoice.'

-The Holy Father

In time, everything will become associated with them.
You walk through the supermarket and you see packets of their favourite snacks that remind you of their nicknames for you.
You hear their favourite songs on the radio.
You associate colours and street signs with them.

One day, you will walk down the street and you will listen to the birds chirping and see the colours of your surroundings, and you will no longer associate.
You will see things for what they are again, and you will feel deeply again.

If you were able to see the things that I have seen and feel the things I have felt, you would not judge me so quickly for not being your standard of 'normal.'

LIMERANCE / (ˈlɪmɪrəns) /

noun

1. A psychological a state of mind resulting from romantic attraction, characterised by feelings of euphoria, the desire to have one's feelings reciprocated, etc.

Sometimes, and most times, you can have hope for something or someone, that never pans out. That is the way of life after all. We don't always get what we want, but that doesn't mean that we should ever stop wishing. I have hoped for certain things and people for over half a decade that in my mind I knew would never happen, but I had the small sliver of hope in the back of my mind that made me believe. It somehow gave me a sense of purpose, as if to kill off the hope was somehow killing off a piece of me too. Some people are of the mind that if you do not have high expectations then you can never be disappointed, but I am of the mind that having hope will make you alive again. One day something or someone will come into your life and extend a hand and say, 'this will make you love again'.

After having my hope shattered so many times on opportunities and people, I started to close myself off again. I didn't want to race ahead again and feel things for something that would end up in ruin. After all, they say Hope breeds eternal misery. But does it? I started to think it might be true, but then the universe turned up for me and reminded me that I'd been waiting patiently for results and here they are, the path that I was on was going to be the right path. I think the spirits must have laughed at my reaction because lord knows, I raced to be a fool again. I was invigorated with a Hope I have never had for life before. A Hope that sustained me and awoke me from a monotonous path that held no purpose. Suddenly, I believed again. I was inspired to be the best that I could be. Even if it doesn't pan out, I will be okay, because it reminded me of what it feels like to believe and feel again. I have hope for something that I wish every day to come true, and if not, I will always be my Hope.

Abigail Remmer

Tell me the place
Tell me the time.
I will always be there.

-Waiting

I need to detach, but I just can't when I see you standing there.

-Obsession starts with the need to run away from yourself

Gloss these scars over with your love.

-Healer of Hearts

I don't care what you do; I want to know who you are.
I want to know your dreams, your fears, and doubts.
I want to know if you will risk looking like a fool for love,
because if you will, then so will I.

-An Invitation

When you walk across the room, my heart beats to a different rhythm.
I am suddenly underwater and gasping for air.
Every mile we are apart, my heart cannot recover from its normal tune.
I think I have died.

-Palpitations

Leave me to my own devices.
Let me smell your scent from miles away,
and dream of your legs wrapped around me.
Your stare can never put the fear in me.

I know you'll lift me higher than the sun,
your lips will taste of honey and magic.
I know you'll understand.
It's got to be wrong before it's right.

-Animals

I have spent my whole adolescence missing you.
I feel homesick.
Why did you tell me you were glad you met me
when you had no intention of showing me so?

-False hopes

All littered in shades of Origami.
Save those little pearls and free yourself,
she's not right for you,
you think about it too.
Take a look in the mirror,
can you say you're where you wanted to be?
Don't be mad,
don't be frustrated.
Not everyone can understand you like me.
Does your mommy know you still cry for her?

-Origami

Abigail Remmer

You keep me under your spell,
you know I love you as well.
Failing between my eyes,
it comes as no surprise.
I know, I know
you're always good.

-Love Witch

You're my Heathcliff, my Rochester.
I am standing on the dark and windy moors
waiting for you, my gothic hero.
My Byronic love affair.
I am sat in the glow of my car lights on these wet hills,
just waiting...

-I forgive you

Abigail Remmer

I tried to keep it subtle
I tried to make you aware.
It kills me inside that you feel,
that you feel you shouldn't care.
I tried my very best
to keep our relationship the same,
it hurts even more,
that you don't remember my name.
I couldn't hold it in any longer
I was just so proud,
but I'm just another girl,
another face in the crowd.

-I never wanted your autograph

You have a strange, almost otherworldly glow about you, my dear.

-Heavenly creature

Abigail Remmer

They ask me why I sleep so much.
It is because my heavy eyelids want to protect us.
Dreaming is our only haven,
and I won't let it get away.

-*Affections of the heart*

We didn't have to say a word to each other.
It hung in the air.
Once a beautiful musk, now a rotting fester.

-Pineapple and pain

You look me down, faceless.
I can't sense your bloodlust, faithless.
I feel your fear I feel the emotional void.
Who are you really why are you so paranoid?

-Algorithm

Your voice is my favourite sound in this world.
It makes my knees shake.
As soon as I felt the vibration of your vocal cords
travelling through the air into my delicate ears;
I was done for.

-Sonorous

Abigail Remmer

I am light.
I am Hope.
I am a newness
that believes
without seeing.

I'm blinded.
Lost in the dark.
Why are you so far away from me?
My feet turn to cement.
I'm blinded.
Lost in the dark.
You recoil and glamour out of sight,
but I hear the burning of bone in the night.
Please, let me go this time.
I'll be the golden glitter in the sky,
I will be waiting on the other side.

-Hero

Abigail Remmer

There is no need to say sorry
you are who you are.
All I do is for you,
I know they do not want to see us together.
I feel overwhelmed,
from this lust so heavy and blue.

-Chloroform

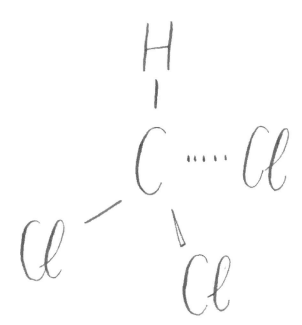

I don't think you ever realised what made you who you are.
Oh, to be a brave warrior.
We should be dancing with the angels.
You have the presence of a lover,
with the face of a mother.

-*Chloe*

Abigail Remmer

Your effervescence is undeniable;
your presence reminds me of joy.
You have me talking like Jay Gatsby;
your eyes are my greenlight.

-Old Sport

I feel my bones crack and croak when I'm in your arms,
I didn't do what you think I did.
I'll tell you all the things you'd like to hear,
I would chase you until the end of the night.

-System Glitch

Abigail Remmer

Your middle name should be Hope.

-Restart

You brought me back from the dead.
I want to serve you.

-Alive and bright

HOPE [hohp]

noun

1. the feeling that what is wanted can be had or that events will turn out for the best: *to give up hope.*
2. a particular instance of this feeling: *the hope of winning.*
3. grounds for this feeling in a particular instance: *There is little or no hope of his recovery.*
4. a person or thing in which expectations are centered: *The medicine was her last hope.*
5. something that is hoped for: *Her forgiveness is my constant hope*

verb (used with object), **hoped, hoping.**
6. to look forward to with desire and reasonable confidence.
7. to believe, desire, or trust: *I hope that my work will be satisfactory.*

verb (used without object), **hoped, hoping.**
8. to feel that something desired may happen: *We hope for an early spring.*
9. *Archaic.* to place trust; rely (usually followed by *in*).

ORIGIN OF HOPE
Before 900; (noun) Middle English; Old English *hopa;* cognate with Dutch *hoop*, German *Hoffe*; (*v.*) Middle English *hopen*, Old English *hopian.*

You are my Hope.

Your smile is prettier than any sunset I've ever experienced.

-Screensaver

Abigail Remmer

Breath into my breath,
I will breathe into yours.
Feel you cascading into me,
your life Force flowing into
my body with extravagance
and purpose.
You make me immortal.

-A certain kind of courage

Lust, take off Love's mask and show me who you are.

-Hope breeds eternal misery?

Abigail Remmer

If I leave you to your own devices,
you will not hurt me.
If I fantasise about your love from me from a distance,
you can never know.
If I dream about us in infinity,
we will never be apart.

-Shooting Star

You are my Hope.

Sorry to keep you waiting,
I just wanted to say
that you can stay here,
I won't turn you away.
Let me ingest your pollen
let my eyelids flutter with sin.
You can keep the engine running,
I want to see your wicked grin.

-Moaning Howl

Abigail Remmer

I think I have found my soulmate.
I'm terrified of going day by day without you,
of having to pick and choose between people
who could only ever be a quarter of the
glittering galaxy that is your eyes.
I think I have found my soulmate.

-*Align*

I want to be your voyeur.
Please my gorgeous Sir,
let her stay,
I want to be your voyeur.

-Dark academia

Abigail Remmer

I'm looking
for signs
and symbols
in the walls
and the cracks.

It's simple.

Your
eyes
flow
like
summer.

-Digital

Trust me I can be by your side.
Show me is it, Mr Jekyll or Mr Hyde?

-Memories of the future

I want to walk in our garden forever,
tasting the sweetness from the fruit
that was rejected from years gone by.
The rare juice of a paradise,
spritzing from the evolved seed.

The naked truth from the lilt of your voice,
that rests on the floor of my tongue.
The tempting duality of your psyche
that reveals and toils inside my womb.
The neural pathways that electrify from
the oasis that your summer brings.

We can hide away behind the billowing
curtains that shelter your fears.
You can hold me down and violate
my sense of justice.
Everything that I hold dear.

Your kiss like fresh rosemary and elderflower,
that sweet saliva that drips down and chokes.
Your balance is a healer that leads
me through the lost and hazy days
of the scorched sands.

The lips, the eyes, the dream;
like cool water that eases my pain.
You are a beautiful lie that hides me
from the honest light.

-Love like a sunset

You are a present from the universe made of stardust and light fractures and love.
I am ready to receive you and start our lives together.
I knew it the moment I set my eyes on you.
You are my soulmate.
My reason to be.

-Love.

Sunset canal, please set me free
for the sunrise will come too soon.
I want to hold you close to me
and tell stories of you to the moon.
I wish I could say that our futures will align,
but I'm afraid I'm deluded too.
So, please hold me close and be mine
until the dusk softly kisses you.

-Leiden

I sense loneliness in you,
a hunger that I can feed.
Why don't we be sad together?

-The Dark Side

You're a cold killer King with a fire in your eyes.

You told me that we would never be together.
Not under this moon.
Not in this lifetime.

I think that is now a blessing.
You can no longer suck my blood by surprise.
I was so addicted to the thrill,
to the chase and to the kill.

I realise now that you are not the cosmic entity that breathed real life
into me.
You are the nightmare that comes to me in the daylight.
The tortuous 3 am trauma of the awakened.

Yet he is the spring that comes with the summer.
I was yours just as much as you are now hers.
Your words were my oxygen,
now fettered smoke signals.

Your Neptune Azure eyes were my guiding light,
now just a skies edge.
It would have hurt me more to conceal that which was true,
So, I confessed and abandoned and unloaded.

I guess the sinners were destined to drift.

-Untrustworthy thorns

Your voice is the human equivalent of petrichor.

-Tongue

My soul has been yearning for you my entire life.
My soul has fought championships in preparation for your war.
My soul leapt out of my body and pointed at you.

-Hallucination

I like to think I never chose you.
The universe put you in my path and after that,
I could not turn back.

-A little girls Hope turns to dust

Your long and lithe body encompasses my space,
every single pointed bone in your spine is there for me to trace.
You are so heavenly and pretty when you appear to be so unreal,
spitting in my face and causing heartache is a reason for me to kneel.

Don't look at me like that you lost and lonely boy.

I am sorry, I know you are quiet and tired but I feel you, all the same,
if you let me in, I will wear you out and I will make you tame.

I can't help but laugh.

You grin wistfully at the sun as if it is there to help you.

Your brain is always distorted it craves deranged discipline,
your cries for help are the eyes of a child yet to me so full of sin.
You kill yourself with burdensome change; your mind is your own
worst enemy,
your stained glass skin shatters into fragments, which flitter down
into me.
She thinks you really love her but she makes you feel sick,
I know you are just as curious, the crowded room is there for you to
pick.
You see yourself as a man that has a penchant for murderous deeds,
I see you as an angel with a battle of dangerous and toxic needs.
I will sit you down and comb your dark and greasy, wretched hair,
I will kiss you on the neck and suckle at your blood until you really
care.
You sink into your twisted mask and pray to God for it to end.

But it will never end.

I will never quit, not until you fight back.
Please… at least fight back.

-The devil laughs at the hearts of lovers; he is a real gentleman.

You'll have to reject me harder.
Hope doesn't believe you.

-Hoffnung und Himmel

I have fought the good fight for too long.
I have been shot and pierced by the hands of love and time.
I have put down my battle axe and my poetry, and I have resigned.
But then like the wildest wind, you come blustering through me,
and I think to myself,
perhaps one more war cannot hurt.

-Battlefield

When I see you in a room,
I delude myself into believing
that you see me as infinitely
as I see you;
like constellations and magic.
But that is only in my dreams.

-Hope begins to shatter

I thought you were a God or maybe some fallen angel.
But you are just like the rest of them.
You are a lost and lonely little boy,
who is waiting for his father to tell Him
to go up and beyond.

-Reimagining

I was so desperate not to lose you this time that in doing so I lost you. I am persistently idiotic in my attempts to be persistent.

-Rehearsing change

You are the biggest plot twist there ever was.
The villain of my dreams that I write stories about.
The crusader king comes to save a little girl from nightmares and ugly lies.
I am in equal amounts in love with you, as I am afraid of you.
I have always loved the darkness.

-A *Tin Man*

You are my Hope.

You are an ecstatic piece of the universe.
I wish I was a special as you.

-*Discovery*

You are art.
A real-life masterpiece.
I need a piece of you.
You're so cool,
everyone wants to be you.
I want to be you.
Your girl wants to be you.
Your parents want to be you.
Your friends want to be you.
The transparent lunch bag
blowing in the wind
wants to be you.
The hummingbird on the branch
wants to be you.
You are art.
A real-life masterpiece.
I need a piece of you.
I need to be you.

-So cool

You look stunning, is that suit new?
How about I buy us a drink?
Why don't we dance the night away?
You're mesmerising I want to know you more.

This is madness.
Yes, I'm fine, thank you.
Actually, I've been better.
You're cute but I'm not really in the mood now,
I think I will just write poetry about you instead.

-Lonely Hearts Club

What's wrong mein Liebling,
does nobody over here love you?
Do you feel lonely,
do you need me to love you?
Hey don't give up,
you are giving your all.
Don't worry you're not old yet,
you don't feel like a failure.
You have a job to die for,
it makes lots of money.
Oh, honey,
It's funny that you only care about money,
well if that's the case you don't need me to make you happy.

Do you feel shortchanged,
you should work harder.
Is this place not what you thought it would be?
Do you feel angry?
Why don't you twist the knife a little after you stick it in?
We can't be done,
well, why don't you jot down a list of all the issues inside your brain?
I know that someone loves you,
I know that someone cares,
I'll make you happy happy,
so, something good can come from all those stares.

-Adapter

These lights have failed me.
You have failed me.
Why do I keep doing this to myself?
Sprinting across the finish line
before you even see me.
The real me.
I think that I am lost.
I think that I have been
waiting in the dark
all my life.

-Bronze sparklers

You don't have to carry me anymore,
I have found my purpose.
You don't have to hesitate anymore,
my energy is limitless.
When you call to me, I will be ready,
I will wash your feet and feed you grapes.
I will forgive you when your tongue messes up,
I will forgive you when you betray me again.
You will forgive me when I bring you down
and steal your golden crown.

-Death and the state

You are my Hope.

Like fairytale and fallacy,
I have fallen in love
with what can never be.

-Melancholia

Oh, baby, I want to snort you up my nose,
feel you invade all my senses,
feel every nerve in my body become ecstatic and inflamed.
I can see the danger in your eyes,
I can already feel the deepness of the cuts.
I'm falling too fast,
I think I'm seeing angels.

-Cyber Sex

Your name has become an emotion to me.
It has become an aura to me.
Navy blue and forest green.
The sound of your voice is the sound of my beating heart.
Just as my bones creak and my blood rushes,
I have never felt more alive than with you.
Alive in a way that truly matters.

I want your cigarette scented fingers
red from furious typing and stained
from copious amounts of coffee.
The books beside your bed do not
receive the attention that you give to
your dream.
I wish for you to look at me
the way I look at you, all starry-eyed and
hopeful,
with the vast array of the
galaxies swimming in the hazel pools
of your soul.
I just can't push a tear out for you.
You give me too much Hope.

-Big Data

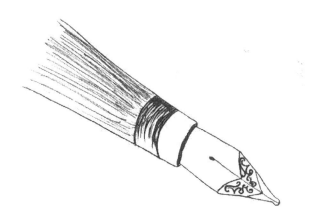

I have only ever felt pain in my life.
Perhaps that's why I am addicted to it.
You bring me the best pain imaginable,
you feed me so well.

-A certain kind of sadness

I'm not an addict. I can quit anytime I want.

-Denial

Whenever you're away from me, I feel static.
Whenever we are together, I feel more absence than joy.
It is as if your presence is a painful reminder that this dream of mine
is just a forgotten fantasy.
You know that I am a fool, I dream of our hearts merging
but our stars seem crossed,
and when the night is gone,
I feel lost.

-Dynamic

Abigail Remmer

You made me feel so small.
I am in love with who you used to be.
I want you back.
I am calling for help and you don't come to me.
All I want is for you to come to me.
I know that you don't care
you don't care about my cries for help.
I must let you go.
How do I push someone I love over a cliff edge to save myself?

-*Standing at the edge*

I stood on a step stool and put my heart on a bracket shelf.
I felt impaired; I felt my heart was not to give.
It's like you heard me and you knew, and you came out of nowhere
and blew into my life.
It's been a long time coming but now I feel your touch,
I know that I can finally close my eyes and dream peacefully.

-Love starts with a Hello

Downtrodden and cast aside, I was a fool for thinking that my thoughts would change my life.

I was a fool for thinking that you would arrive and change my life, but you did.

A tall dark handsome man with an arched eyebrow, and a wicked smile and hands covered in blood, glided to me and revived me.

I can feel the pounding of my battle drum

beating

beating

beating

beating just for you.

You stemmed the bleeding and pulled the tourniquet tighter, hazily looking into your eyes I now see what's real.

All this time, you've been right around the corner.

-Crimson static

You came to me like the crash of the waves,
your virginal spirit croaks and clashes and caves.
I thought I was living but, in my heart, I truly know,
I'd been dead for years, and I'd never let it show.

-Infusion

Run back and suddenly appear
it was if the world has turned
and left me here.
Belonging.
I feel you descend upon me
where did you go for so long, baby?
We stare for hours
we do not know what to say.
So save your voice
and grasp my hips.
I want you desperate and raw.
Take me, hostage,
and craft me anew.
I see you with the eyes of my soul.
I am overflowing with you.

-Did you go somewhere, mein Liebling?

You melt away the darkness;
you break bones
and cure catastrophes.
You disintegrate mountains
and craft kidnapped hearts
into romantic soliloquies
that rival ancient philosophy.
You create firelight
for all to see.
You create Hope
deep within me.

-Life is but a dream!

Pluck my flower
after I have bloomed.
My delicate petals
are pastel, pink, and plentiful.

Pluck my flower
after I have bloomed.
Your dexterous hands
are brash, brave and beautiful.

Your lips deserve more than what
my hazy mind can conjure up.
Your mouth could be the altar
that shows me a new way to pray.

-The ache for you is growing

You are more passionate,
more intense
more intelligent
than I could have ever Hoped for.
I want to commit every sin
that you want to commit.
You flitter around like a bumblebee,
pollinating beauty.
Grow me in your garden of love;
sow your seeds in this patch of passion
and let the sun feel jealous of your radiance.
I need you like night needs day.
I need you like life itself.

-Strategy

If you do not look at me
If you do not witness me
If you do not feel me
If you do not *really* see me
do I exist?
And if I don't exist then why am I here?

-Would you live for me?

This unfinished business can go on no longer.
This rare madness is very unbecoming of you.
Yet, I know your loveliness sees our flesh blend as one.
Your tender hands hold the power.
I am fed up of the overthinking
f*** me like you mean it.
I cry for what cannot be,
you and me,
in eternity.

-Cover my body like snow

You warned me from the beginning, but I didn't listen.
I wanted to know you.
I wanted to put myself in your path.
I wanted you to be a part of my world.
You are smart, sensual, crafty and even a little dangerous.
Your physical absence pays no mind to the hand that reaches out for
you every morning.
My senses are vibrating.
My lungs are heavy.
Come back soon.
My heart can only take so much.

-Running off my desires

Abigail Remmer

Driving along the roads
the sun hits my windscreen,
I'm blinded by the view.
Oh, mein Liebling,
it made me think of you.

-Sunshine on the way home

My feelings for you are a hurricane.
I cannot stop thinking about you.
It feels as though you are a
cat with a ball of string.
Yet the ball is my heart, and
your claws want to puncture
its squishy and rubbery texture.
You are deceptively strong for
such as frail feline.
You may hurt me, but I don't care.
I'd rather mean nothing to you
than feel nothing at all.
Your pain feels like Heaven.

-You bring me joy in a way I have never felt before

Abigail Remmer

You are as dark and as magical
as the starry crash of midnight.
I will be lost forever
until you find me again.

-Van Gogh

I can still hear your heart
beating thousands of miles away.
My love travels oceans,
tears cities apart and
sets lost souls free.

-Du bist der Himmel auf Erden für mich.

There is no algorithm that could understand you.
You hold endless and valued secrets.
The softness of those secure sshh's
are like the way you delicately form your S's.
You're not a statistic, a burden, or a piece of data.
You are not an algorithm.
You are skin and sin
and the end of my world,
and I *really* want you.

-Mode

The moon wishes it was as full as you make me feel.
Everything starts just as everything ends.
I overthink when you're not around to keep me focused.
You will leave, and I will have convinced myself to sweetly resist you,
and you'll have to infect me all over again.
Shout my name to the stars and blush and quiver under the
moonlight.
Let me lure you into staying a little longer.

-Dalliance at Dawn

I feel your large hands on my back.
I feel the blood blooming into your rosy cheeks,
and your emerald eyes glimmering with Hope.
You are my end and my beginning.

-Renaissance

I cannot bear a world without you.
I want to live in your ecosystem.
The need for you is as hot, impatient and angry
as an alien bursting through the chest of a young
woman on a white and blue spaceship.
I cannot contain myself.
I splash the bathtub water in frustration
and watch it slosh over the side like an excited tide.
Don't you see baby?
We are it.

-King of Swords

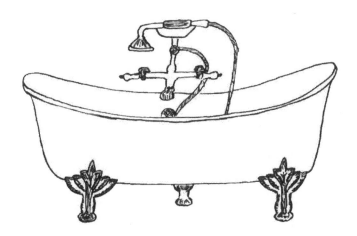

Dear Mein Liebling,

I will pluck the stars from the sky and put them into your palms.
Just like us, they will cross and divide the line,
but they will sparkle and shine, forever thine.
I will cut them up with nimble fingers
and place them into your tired eyes.
Those kind eyes that shatter my soul and disintegrate my might.
Just as Romeo said, 'Did my heart love till now,
for I never saw true beauty until this night.'
I would quote a thousand plays and sonnets if you asked me to,
with your vision keepers now so full of green and midnight blue,
the spinning pearls that hold the universe now so bold and new.
You can sleep peacefully knowing that what you hoped is true,
the love that I have is infinite and eternally for you.
Always.

-Romance

I hate being in love with a person that doesn't exist anymore.

Perhaps we will never end up together.
Sometimes the back and forth can be so exhausting it is almost nauseating.
Perhaps it is too late to be happy with you.
Perhaps you do not realise that my pain can easily resurface.
You always wish you can do better and be better, but I know no one better than you.
It is my choice to let you suffocate me.
The pain I receive will be my punishment.
A punishment I do not deserve, but one that I will seek.

-Reality can be the harshest punishment of all

I am dehydrated, weary and broken.
This desert has scorched me to smithereens.
But I cannot quit,
not until I receive my miracle.
I am only a second away.

The energy is charged from the synapses of my mind,
drip-by-drip all immeasurably refined.
This joke of my reality is laughing insane.
But the truth of the matter is,
it's always my brain.

-I started a joke

Oh, my dark and dangerous Sir, I don't want to let you go.
Please don't make me open my shutters and let you go.
The twinkling beams of your eyes will light the way for me,
forevermore.

I don't feel normal.
I haven't been to the North for a while.
I haven't been home for a while.
I can't defend this piece of territory.
I can't smile my way through this forgotten story.
Everyone has left me behind and I have lost my maker.
I felt nervous and scared.
I am my own heartbreaker.

-North Star

You are a kind killer.
You have granted me mercy at least.

-Apologies for the way you are

Your smile fills my soul with warmth.
You are the beginning and end of every thought.
I feel my senses dying with overload when you look at me,
that wolfish grin kills me in a way that matters.

-Weak knees and achy cheeks

Dominant and clinical.
Oh, my love, I'll let you bend me that way.
In the stillness and the silence, I can feel your energy.
I can smell the scent of blood orange on your skin.
The fruity aroma blends and blurs with the hypnotic stench of ash, and sin.

You remind me of a well-sculpted Parisian building; magnificent, cultured, even a little wise.
If stone and brick could be hot and exciting yet smoky and beige, it would look and feel like you.
Powdery blue skies and clouds like angel wings envelop that building like my love envelops you.

When the puffy white slowly turns to black and blue, the green shimmer of the GO light will flicker off the body of bone like the olive ovals of your eyes.
The sparkling stars will spit out their pearls of light onto the midnight blanket and dance in the glow of your soul.

If I only had this moment, where the shadow of the sun illuminates your canvas, I would remember that scene every day for the rest of my life.
With your art and your pastel paradise of a heart, I'm going to be a better person because of you.

-Viennese Valentine

Flick your cigarette onto my skin and light me up.
My body is alert, but my mind is still dreaming of you.
The first footfall makes me dizzy; I feel the pressure in my head like
the pressure I put onto you.
I needed a remedy, and you entered like a doctor.
You are the salvation that heals.
You are my new supplier.

-Higher than the sky

I juice the hell out of our encounters.
I end up overstaying my welcome, and I wake up feeling dirty.
Sometimes, there are 5 to 6 versions of me all standing around your
bed and fighting to see who will soak your love in tonight.
Will you let me be absurd with you?

I burst at the seams.
I admire your rosy cheeks in the neon lowlight of the dancefloor.
You're so in love with me until you find out who I really am.
A mess when undressed and harsh in tone, you're hot to the touch,
I'm sad and alone.
You've got a girl now, so I don't care, it's okay
I hate myself too,
it's only fair.

-I Hope you're not normal

You run until you vomit.
You write until you cry.
You cry until you feel.
You work until you tire.
You laugh until you ache.
You think until you die.
You're going to be a success.
You're going to be the damn best.
You won't settle for the rest.
You regulate.
You discipline.
You mentor.
You heal.
You motivate.
You dream as big as you can dream.
You love as much as you can love.
You kill me with silence.
You kill me with just one look.
You revive me with endless light.
You revive me with boundless Hope.
You may never know what you did for me.

You didn't come to me.
You didn't save me from the pain.
You didn't cause the pain.
You didn't stop it either.

-Are you at fault?

We seem to talk and talk but to no consequence.
You don't want to play this game.
Too greedy, too violent and too aggressive.
You work so deep, so enriched in a chapter of your life that will be soon forgotten.
I blinded myself to your hot confession, but you lit something within me, whilst you stayed my hand.
Hold back the darkness.
Hold back the sadness.
Hold back the fear darling it's just a war.

-Slow your mind

I am stunned, I see you standing there.
You take my self-control.
I don't put up a fight, I know your heart is kind.
Your face flushes when we are near,
but you recede with a fullness of fear.
We are passing ships in the night

This Hope is a red herring.

It's okay, I will try again.
Another arrow in the wolf's back
can only make it stronger,
even if the pain is greater than it was before.
The edges and curves of your soul
derive pleasure from deep within me.

I don't really know you at all.

Why do you let everyone in but me?
Even if Heaven and Hope came together
and blended with my energy like a godly elixir,
you would still pass me in the night.
Perhaps this time, I will give up the fight.

Oh, strike me down.
This Hope is a goddamn red herring.

Close your tired eyes, press the power button and shut it all down.
Let your mind wander to free skies full of blue and puffy white, and
cherubs playing harps and violins.
Let your mind believe in this, just as I have every single second of
every single day since you shot me with your arrow.
Hold back the fear and spit the regret-filled vodka from your mouth
like a river.
Use it as gasoline for the cigarette between your fingers, and stub the
rolled-up death note onto the f***ers that told you that you're time-
limited.
You say to me you are happy so many times I have soon come to
believe it, but your hurt hazel eyes tell me differently.
You are a simple boy with a smile like the September Summer, and
passion like Heaven's Hope.
I don't want our kiss to become cold, so please do not wait outside
any longer on your own.
Resurrect me with the crash of your violation, take my appendices
and knead them into your design.
If I press my hand to my heart, I feel a gaping hole.
The red right hand you showed me long ago is dripping with the
signals I sent to you.
There is no pulse, no beat, and no life.
It lies with you and your hot, iridescent globes.
This is my story but if you had given me the chance,
I would have let you be the main character.
"If he loved with all the powers of his puny being, he couldn't love as
much in eighty years as I could in a day."
Sometimes I think that is true.
The passion I hold for you could ignite into a fiery explosion of self-
love and self-betterment, instead of this derelict display of lust.
I will let you go. I will let you both be happy.
I want to see you thrive and feel a fullness of joy that glows to the
gods. Maybe you and I cannot eat on the same table together, but
that's okay.
If you come back to me, then I will recede into amazement and
knowing, but if not, thank you for coming into my life and making
me realise that I cannot live the life I have been living.
I need to save myself this time.

You walk into the unknown.
You help everybody but yourself.
Did you long for me? Miss me?
You are guided by the light and
the sweet realisation that we are
each other's truths.
You found me waiting for you,
my arms outstretched.
Were you lonely walking in the desert
on your own, my Messiah.
We are ignorant of everything around us
and the rush inside me has missed you.
I long for a new beginning.
Perhaps that new beginning starts with you.
When I look at you, I know I am not alone.
We wander these brown sands together.
I could weep with joy.
You brought me back to myself.

Printed in Great Britain
by Amazon